The Coup – A Play of Revoluti

A funeral oration for President Eddie Jones; a precarious
military takeover with trigger-happy squabbling factions:
Mustapha Matura's farcical, fictional coup, set in an
independent Trinidad and Tobago, swings with the fluid
language and magical lyricism of the Caribbean and explores
the chimerical quality of nationhood where foreign money
overpowers dreams.

The Coup premièred at the Royal National Theatre in the
Cottesloe on 18 July 1991.

Mustapha Matura was born in Trinidad and came to England
in 1961. His plays include: **As Time Goes By** (1971) which
won both the George Devine and John Whiting Awards; **Nice**
(1973) premièred at the Almost Free Theatre and revived at
Riverside Studios, Hammersmith in 1980; **Play Mas** (1974)
Royal Court, London transferred to the West End, seen in
Chicago (1981) and won the *Evening Standard* Most Promising
Playwright Award; **Rum an' Coca Cola** (1976) Royal Court
and off-Broadway; **Independence** (1979) toured by Foco
Novo; **Welcome Home Jacko** (1979) staged at the Factory,
London by the Black Theatre Co-operative which Matura
had co-founded in 1978 with the director Charlie Hanson
and which presented **Another Tuesday** and **More, More**
(1979); **A Dying Business** (1980) and **One Rule** (1981)
both at Riverside Studios; **Meetings** (1982) directed by the
author at Hampstead Theatre following New York première
in 1981; **Trinidad Sisters** (1988) Tricycle Theatre, London.
Many of his plays have been seen in major cities in the USA
– notably **Playboy of the West Indies**, first staged by Oxford
Playhouse (1984) and seen on BBC (1985).

by the same author

Play Mas
Independence
Meetings

The Coup

A Play of Revolutionary Dreams

Mustapha Matura

Methuen Drama

Methuen Modern Play

First published in Great Britain as a paperback original in the
Methuen Modern Plays series in 1991 by Methuen Drama, Michelin
House, 81 Fulham Road, London SW3 6RB and distributed in the
United States of America by HEB Inc., 361 Hanover Street,
Portsmouth, New Hampshire NH 03801-3959

Copyright © 1991 Mustapha Matura
The author has asserted his moral rights.

ISBN 0-413-65260-2

A CIP catalogue record for this book is available
from the British Library.

The front cover is based on an image by Michael Mayhew from a
photograph of Norman Beaton. The photograph of Mustapha Matura
on the back cover is by Michael Mayhew.

Typeset in 10/11pt Linotron Baskerville
by Hewer Text Composition Services, Edinburgh
Printed and bound in Great Britain
by Cox & Wyman Ltd, Cardiff Road, Reading

The Coup – A Play of Revolutionary Dreams was premièred at the Royal National Theatre in the Cottesloe on 18 July 1991, with the following cast:

Archbishop	Oscar James
President Edward Francis Jones	Norman Beaton
Mikey Jones	Lennie James
Lieutenant le Grange	Stefan Kalipha
Lieutenant Chan	Gordon Case
Christopher Columbus	T-Bone Wilson
Monk	Marc Matthews
Captain	Lenny Aljernon-Edwards
Native Priest	Oscar James
Major Ferret	Jeffery Kissoon
Sergeant Fitzroy Emmanuel Allyne (Black Lightning)	Tony Armatrading
Soldier	Lenny Aljernon-Edwards
First Workman	T-Bone Wilson
Second Workman	Marc Matthews
First Nun	Maureen Hibbert
Second Nun	Josephine Melville
Guard of Honour	T-Bone Wilson, Lenny Aljernon-Edwards, Marc Matthews
Arawaks	Josephine Melville, Maureen Hibbert

Directed by Roger Michell
Designed by William Dudley
Lighting by Rick Fisher

Note: This script went to press before rehearsals of **The Coup**. The punctuation used in the script reflects the flow of the spoken text.

Scene One

The altar of a cathedral, bright sunlight streaming through a large stained-glass window, to shine on an elaborate dark wood, half-opened, purple satin-draped coffin, surrounded by large lighted candles, in the centre of the cathedral. 'My Way' is being played by lone tenor pan player. There is a guard of honour of four services. Taped music changes to processional fanfare. **Archbishop** *enters carrying a crucifix, on flagpoles the national flag, palm branches on walls.* **Archbishop** *goes centre. Makes sign of the cross.*

Archbishop Let us pray, comrades (*Bows head.*) in the midst of life, there is death, an so it is we are gathered here today, heads of state, diplomats, distinguished guests from all corners of the globe, fellow strugglers for justice an ordinary people, to pray, pay tribute, an give thanks for, the father of our nation, Edward Francis Jones, we pray his soul has a safe journey through the seven temples of Ahab an Mayab, and is received into the hands of our Lord, there, to sit on his right hand, according to the tridentine traditions, of Trinidad an Tobago. We pay tribute to the man, Edward Francis Jones, Eddie to his friends, who, by all accounts, had quite normal boydays for a young man of his ilk, being able to tief mangoes with impunity, bathe naked in the rain, without reprimand, let down working people bicycle tyres, an run off laughing, with a benign shake of the head from the unfortunate cyclist, but who would have thought, those days, climbing trees, pitching marbles, catching tadpoles, playing stick-em-up, cricket an football on the back streets of Port of Spain, would be Eddie's preparations, preparations, that would one day, lead to him arguing, outsmarting, bullying, begging, blackmailing, cussing, mamaguying, an finally daring, the British into granting us independence, who would have thought, in the far corners of the British Empire, namely the pubs of Earl's Court and Hampstead, the bars of Bush an Broadcasting

House, Caribbean, Indian and African, scholars and politicians would be asking themselves the same questions and coming to different answers, how do we gain our independence, do we beg for it or do we fight for it, in other words, can you make an omelette without breaking any eggs, Gandhi, Nehru, Kenyatta, Nkruma, Bustamante, Jagan, Ho, all asked those questions, Eddie Jones, Trini to the bones, choose to negotiate, was he right or was he wrong, history will have to judge him, but the dream of independence he inherited, on the back streets of Port of Spain, was to become a reality on the corridors of Lancaster House, some people criticised him at the time for succeeding, but as far as I know, he never held that against them, for that, we pay tribute to Trinidad, Trinidad, did I say, yes, because it's Trinidad a mean, we made him, but a nation is a funny ting, yer know, it could make you or break you, especially, when it made up of every race, colour, creed, religion an sect, with a lust an greed, to be bigger an better than their neighbours by any means possible, who could govern an make them live together, nobody, but for every moment there is the man, Edward Francis Jones, was that man, I en saying he was a saint or perfect, you know, he didn't tell everybody he was devaluing de dollar, some people made a killing, some of us got burnt, but I an I survived, I didn't agree with his social security plan, an I told him so, in many episcopal letters, I still say if you give Trinidadians too much money, dey en go work, but he showed me the unemployment figures, it was either that, or more armed robberies, it's not easy, now we have a new master, I would only say one thing to them, Trinidadians don't like nobody to tell dem wat to do yer know, they don't like it at all, let us pray, (*Bows head.*) Lord we deliver unto you for safe keeping the father of our nation, an hope you take better care of him than we did, amen, those of you wishing to back your last respects may do so now, while we beat, hymn seven seven seven, lucky seven, alright, everybody, lighten up, ner,

Takes out a splif lights it. Sound of African drumming. Lights.

Scene Two

A prison cell on the island of Trinidad. In it the **President**, *sixty-ish, negro origin, asleep on a bed. There are shouts, screams off, doors banging. He wakes, slowly rises, goes to grill.*

President Officer, officer, I'd like some water, could I have a drink of water, please.

Mikey I'm sorry sir, I don't know if I'm suppose to do that, I'll have to check.

President But I'm,

Mikey Hole on ner, sir, (*Goes.* **President** *paces,* **Mikey** *returns.*) de sergeant say is alright sir, here, (*Tries to put tin cup through bars, it does not pass.*)

President You'll have to open the door.

Mikey I do' know if I suppose to do dat, you know sir, I don't even have de keys, I'll have to go an ask de sergeant again,

President Alright, I'm thirsty.

Mikey *goes, returns.*

Mikey (*unlocking door*) De sergeant say is alright, as long as yer stand with yer back against de wall an I put it down on de floor an step back out, without indulging in any conversation, yer agree,

President I agree,

Mikey Good, because some a dese SLR, does just go off on dey own, especially if there's any struggle,

President I understand,

President *backs to wall, hands up.* **Mikey** *enters, places cup on floor.*

President Thank you,

Mikey No conversation sir, (*Goes out locks door.*) wen yer finish wid de cup tell me, I'll come an get it.

President They think I'll scratch my way out of here, (*Calls out.*) take your time, I'm a slow drinker, (*Sits, drinks slowly.*) it's just what I needed, you can't beat good ole Trinidad water, it's what runs through our veins, eh, that's better, officer, do you know if I'm going to be fed, or is that another part of their master plan to free the world by imprisoning the democratically elected president, of their country,

Mikey I do' know notting bout no food, sir.

President Well, will you go an check with the Sergeant, please,

Mikey I'll ask him later, I'm not suppose to leave my post, you see.

President Well, that's good of you, good discipline, you must have that in life, you in the regiment long,

Mikey I not suppose to talk to you yer know sir,

President But what's,

Mikey Dat's my orders, sir, I could get in trouble,

President Well I wouldn't want you to do that, but there's one thing I'd like you to tell me, if you can, do you know what happen to my wife and children. (*Beat.*) I understand, if you can't tell me, but are they safe, clear your throat if they're safe or bang your rifle on the floor, on the other hand don't bang your rifle, those SLR's does go off, right, (*Beat.*) the British sold us them you know, I wanted us to go for the Kalashnikov 47, but that would have meant having Cuban instructors which would have worried the Americans, besides, the British gave us a interest free loan to buy them, from them, such gentlemen the British although they screwing you, you never lose the feeling you're dealing with gentlemen, so the Foreign Minister, the Defence Minister an the Finance

Minister won that one, it was good to see them talking to each other for a change,

Mikey It's a good rifle,

President What about my family, any,

Mikey Yer trying ter get me in trouble or what,

President I'm sorry, well let's talk about rifles then, what yer think a de armalite, yer test it, I know they send down some high powered ex-Green Berets salesmen, one a them raped a whore on Abercromby Street, I had to sign a presidential amnesty for that, it only cost us a new primary school in Naparima, a library of Tennessee Williams's plays, 5000 sets of Aspen skis, and a Kentucky Fried Chicken franchise, on the roundabout at Barataria, I should know I cut the ribbon myself, there was traffic jams for days, (*Beat.*)

Mikey People like new tings, sir,

President That's what I'm afraid of, if you have a wife an children you'll understand, (*Beat.*)

Mikey I have a child wit a woman, but we not married,

President I see, boy or girl,

Mikey A boy,

President What's his name,

Mikey Ruben,

President It's a nice name for a boy,

Mikey Well, he is a boy,

President I went to school with a feller call Ruben, what was his last name, Garcia, no, Govia, no, de Freitas, that's it, Ruben de Freitas, boy he was always getting me in trouble, Ruben de Freitas, that's him, yer see the ole brain still working, eh,

Mikey It comes from the bible,

President You read the bible a lot,

Mikey That's what it's there for,

President That's right,

Mikey It was one of de twelve tribes of Israel,

President That's good,

Mikey It's part of our heritage, that's all,

President Yes, we inherited a lot of things with colonialism, a foreign dominated economy, some crumbling old buildings, with crumbling old civil servants in them, a police service that was the plaything of a Victorian crank, run a the mill ex-colony thing, (*Beat.*) As well as a loss of our sense of history,

Mikey Yes,

President But after all that, I still say we Trinis did a good job, up to now, (*Beat.*) well at least a have to thank you for one thing,

Mikey What's dat,

President Ruben de Freitas,

Mikey What about de water,

President Two things, then,

Mikey Thank you, sir,

President Do you agree with what they're doing, do you think,

Mikey Sir, I is just a soldier yer know, sir, my job is just to follow orders,

President I accept that, an that's commendable, but do you think what they're doing is right,

Mikey Sir, I'm just a soldier, (*Beat.*) I shouldn't even be talking to you, now, (*Beat.*)

President I just want to know if they safe, (*Beat. Laughs.*) yes, boy, that Ruben de Freitas was trouble, one time he took me on to Mister Brown's land to tief plum, he said he'll stand guard, he see Mister Brown coming down the track an run off an leave me up the tree, Mister Brown made me eat all the plums in my bag, right there an then, all the time cuffing me an saying you shouldn't tief what you can't eat, you ever try to eat plums with somebody cuffing you, (*Beat.*) what's yer woman's name,

Mikey Ursula,

President It's a nice name, my wife's name is Margaret, an my son is John, I named him after Johnny Gomez, the greatest all-rounder this island ever produced, bat an ball Johnny was the best,

Mikey Cricket's not my game,

President That's a shame, you could learn a lot from a game of cricket,

Mikey What's yer other child's name,

President Oh, Stella, after my mother, she's in the entertainment business, fashion shows an modelling, I don't know much about it, young people thing,

Mikey I want my son to be a doctor wen he grow up, or a lawyer, something where he can better himself,

President My boy is having a whale of a time, one minute he wants to be a reggae singer, the next, a biologist who feeds the world, but I think he'll settle for politics,

Mikey (*beat*) What kinda plums dey was,

President Governor,

Mikey *laughs softly.*

President Do you know where they are, (*Beat.*)

Mikey No, sir,

President Can you find out for me, (*Beat.*)

Mikey (*shouts*) Yer finish wit de cup, sir,

President What, yes, thank you,

Mikey Den please stand wit yer back against de wall, while I open this door an take it, an please don't attempt to engage me in any conversation whilst I'm doing it,

President Yes, yes, (*Backing off.*)

Mikey (*enters, rifle aimed, whispers*) I don't have anyting against you, yer know, sir, (*Picks up cup, backs out, locks door.*)

President Thank you, (*Beat.*) how old are you,

Mikey I'm twenty five sir,

President That would put you at, what, 64, right, not bad eh, the year we came to power, the year we gave the people of Trinidad a future to look forward to an they accepted it, some a the boys on the executive committee didn't think we could do it, but we were asking the British for independence, an the people were listening, anybody with eyes, could tell we were on the move to something, even the British couldn't miss it, look, they told us, if your party gets a majority of the seats, we will grant you independence, we won every seat, they left us some damn good administrators to ease us into independence, because quite frankly, we were not prepared, government is a hell of a responsibility, take Sonny Lutchmansingh, Minister of Housing an Local Government, the first day we took office he started calling everybody sir, even the cleaning woman, I had ter take him aside an say, Sonny, it's going to be alright, go an look at a reservoir, we were young then, mostly ex-QRC boys, but we didn't know how the civil service would react to local boys telling them what to do, but we had carefully represented in the government, every racial group, and they held, we learned, as you, go along, you learn, an we did a damn good job, I don't care what anybody says, you make your mistakes as well as your successes,

Mikey My father told me about those meetings, sir,

President Yes,

Mikey Sir, a don't tink dey going ter feed yer, yer know, sir,

President Thank you for telling me that,

Mikey A could get you some more water,

President That would be nice,

Soldier *goes,* **President** *lies down,* **Soldier** *returns,* **President** *backs to wall, hands up.*

Mikey Is all right sir, (*Goes out locks door.*)

President (*drinks*) But don't think we left the British empty handed yer know, no, man, we got them to promise to hand over ownership of the refineries at Pointe Pierre, at a realistic price an by an large they kept their word, give or take a few million, all wireless an telecommunications services, the airport, customs and,

*Shout from down corridor from the Sergeant (***Black Lightning***).*

Black Lightning Attention, down there, officers approaching,

Mikey *comes to attention.*

Calls coming down line from **Lieutenants Chan** *and* **le Grange** *and* **Guards** *on duty.*

Lieutenant Chan Sentry on duty,

Guard 1 Sentry on duty sir,

Lieutenant Le Grange Sentry on duty,

Guard 2 Sentry on duty sir,

Lieutenant Chan Sentry on duty,

Guard 3 Sentry on duty sir,

Lieutenant le Grange Sentry on duty,

Mikey Sentry on duty, sir,

Lieutenant le Grange *(at door)* Shit, it do' have a table or chairs,

Lieutenant Chan Soldier, go an get de table, the Sergeant just put his boots back up on, an bring it here,

Lieutenant le Grange Yer get that,

Mikey Yes, sir,

Lieutenant le Grange And two chairs,

Lieutenant Chan Yer have dat,

Mikey Yes, sir,

Lieutenant Chan What a tell yer,

Mikey Yer told me to go an get the table the Sergeant just put his boots back up on, sir, an bring it back here with two chairs,

Lieutenant Chan I didn't tell you to bring back two chairs, that was Lieutenant le Grange,

Mikey Yes, sir,

Lieutenant Chan Now go an get dem,

Mikey *moves to open door.*

Lieutenant Chan Did I ask you to open the door?

Mikey No, sorry sir,

Lieutenant Chan Now go,

Mikey Yes, sir, *(Goes, returns with table.)*

Lieutenant le Grange What about the chairs,

Mikey A have ter go back fer dem sir,

Lieutenant Chan Hurry up,

Mikey Yes, sir, *(Goes, returns with two chairs.)*

Lieutenant le Grange Now, open the door,

Mikey Yes, sir, (*Does.*)

Two **Lieutenants** *enter the cell, they are both in combat uniform, pistols, carrying papers, folders.* **Lieutenant Chan** *is of Indian origin and* **Lieutenant le Grange** *is of African origin.*

President Have you come to release me, give me news of my family or murder me,

Lieutenant Chan Please be seated Mister President, on the bed,

President Address me as sir, since by your actions you have shown total disrespect for the office an those who elected it,

Lieutenants *position chairs between behind table and bed, sit.*

Lieutenant le Grange Let's get dis over with,

President What have you done with my family,

Lieutenant Chan We will come to them later, first, allow me to introduce ourselves, sir, I am Lieutenant Chan, and my brother officer here is Lieutenant le Grange, we are joint chairmen of the combined armed services committee, an we have been charged with full powers to negotiate the conditions of your release,

President Where is my family,

Lieutenant le Grange Yer didn't hear or what, Lieutenant Chan said we'll come to them later,

Lieutenant Chan (*to* **Lieutenant le Grange**) Take it easy ner. Sir, as I said, Lieutenant le Grange an myself are empowered by the combined armed services committee to,

President I heard what you said, did you hear me,

Lieutenant le Grange The lieutenant heard you sir, I heard you too, we will discuss your family an dem wen we ready, de political progress of our country is more important than the whereabouts of your over-privileged an corrupt family.

Lieutenant Chan (*to* **Lieutenant le Grange**) Yer see you, that's why you an I will never agree, yer call dat easy, I ask yer ter go easy an what yer doing? Sir, what Lieutenant le Grange saying is right, the political progress of our country is much more important than the whereabouts of your over-privileged an corrupt family, at present,

President Well, if that is your argument and I agree, the political progress of our country is more important than my family, in that case I demand you release me and the ministers you arrested, return to your barracks at Chagarumas and place yourselves an the other members of the combined armed services committee under arrest, an,

Lieutenant le Grange A tell yer we shoulda shoot 'im, last night,

Lieutenant Chan Look le Grange, you want ter do dis, or you want me ter do it, because,

Lieutenant le Grange No, no, you do it, you do it,

Lieutenant Chan Right, sir, you don't understand as from last night, the combined armed services committee, declared de formation of a new government to run this country, it was a coup,

President That's what you call it, I call it an attempt by intellectual bullies, to impose their fourth-hand ideas of democracy an terrorise the people of Trinidad and Tobago, at the same time,

Lieutenant le Grange Wat happen to dis man or wat,

Lieutenant Chan Sir,

President Lieutenant, I don't know what they taught you at Sandhurst, but I am sure they taught you a soldier's first duty is to the lawfully elected government of his country, an to stay out of politics,

Lieutenant Chan Sir, there are times when a soldier have to make decisions for the better of all de people,

President Well, he should then resign his commission, and stand for election, put his ideas to the people, an let them decide, Trinidadians not stupid you know,

Lieutenant Chan We know that, sir, that is why we, as officers, took the responsibility on ourselves an decided to liberate the people from your corrupt and oppressive regime,

Lieutenant le Grange Tell 'im ner,

Lieutenant Chan Sir, we did not come here to discuss the outdated rituals of western democracy,

Lieutenant le Grange Not dat, de ting,

Lieutenant Chan I'm getting to dat, sir, you, Edward Francis Jones, has been charged by the combined armed services committee, with, I am now going to read de charges starting with one. One, being a traitor to the people of Trinidad an Tobago, two, of running a corrupt, decadent and oppressive government on behalf of your own family, the corrupt ruling classes of this island, and foreign corporations, four,

President What happen to three,

Lieutenant le Grange Silence,

Lieutenant Chan Is a misprint, three, that since assuming the office of president you opened several Swiss bank accounts where the proceeds of your corruption now exceed 15.2 million dollars, and on foreign trips you have paid visits to brothels, had the use of call girls, an,

President I'm a Trinidadian man,

Lieutenant Chan You seem to be taking this lightly,

President What else can I do, it's lies, lies, all lies, what the man said, oh, yes, an damn lies, what do you expect me to say to the ravings of a pack of fools,

Lieutenant le Grange A told yer dis was a waste of time, let's do it,

Lieutenant Chan Wait ner,

President Lieutenant Chan, I order you to,

Lieutenant Chan Sir, since you are no longer President, I am no longer obliged to obey orders from you, an I have here a confession for you to sign,

President What?

Lieutenant le Grange Tell 'im,

Lieutenant Chan Sir, the combined services armed committee, has agreed to certain conditions, one, that you and your family be allowed to leave the country with no possessions, two, that you live in England or America,

Lieutenant le Grange Where you have property,

Lieutenant Chan I reading this or you, (*Stewps.*) three, and that you do not attempt to return or engage in any political activity involving the Peoples Republic of Trinidad and Tobago. (*Beat.*)

Lieutenant le Grange What yer say,

President What,

Lieutenant le Grange What yer say, yer agree,

President To what,

Lieutenant le Grange To de conditions,

Lieutenant Chan Sir,

Lieutenant le Grange Sir,

President You want my signed confession,

Lieutenant Chan Yes sir, those are the conditions for your release as laid down by the combined armed,

President Lieutenant, I find your conditions an insult to me personally, an to the good people of Trinidad who were kind enough to give you an education in life, no, I will not sign

your confession, the fact that you considered I might, proves
what fools you are, I give you six months at most, before you
begging someone to take over, yer think Trinidad is a parade
ground, yer just tell people do this an they'll do it, no, you tell
your armed services commissars, I refuse, your conditions, like
your charges are the dregs of an excuse, to satisfy your lust for
power, and I repeat, damn lies, what about my family,

Lieutenant Chan Sir, I will convey your remarks to the
combined armed services committee and let you know our
decision, but a think a should warn yer, we serious bout dis
yer know,

President So am I Lieutenant, what about my family,

Lieutenant Chan Yes, now we come to your family, (*To*
Lieutenant le Grange.) you want to deal with this or me,

Lieutenant le Grange I will, what yer want ter know bout
yer family,

President Where are they,

Lieutenant le Grange Dey safe,

President Can I see them,

Lieutenant le Grange We can't let dem out,

President Where are they,

Lieutenant le Grange Dey under de protective custody of de
regiment,

President Why should they need protection,

Lieutenant le Grange Since de take over, de people hear
bout, all de sins an corruption dey committed, there was
crowds and riots outside Governor House, the regiment had
to break it up, law an order is high on our list, so we imposed
a curfew,

President If you can't govern by consent you'll never govern,
I was over-generous as usual, I gave you six months, I give

you weeks, now, I shoulda never send you boys to Sandhurst, that cushy training ground for third world take over specialists, it shoulda been one a the gulags in Siberia to dig snow, an queue for bread, all day, then you woulda know what life is all about, an ter think I spend a whole night in the company of a crude Under-Secretary of State for Overseas Development, at the Mirama Nightclub ter get all yer the scholarships, yer didn't know that did yer, but I thought, what the heck, we must have the best for our boys, what a waste, a curfew, a curfew on the streets of Trinidad, I never thought I'd live to see the day,

Lieutenant le Grange That too, mighten be much longer, either,

President Yes, that, (*Beat.*) do you intend feeding me, or doesn't that come in your KGB manual, for brutalising prisoners,

Lieutenant Chan That is a matter for the combined armed services committee to decide,

Lieutenant le Grange What happen yer do' like de water,

Lieutenant Chan Right now we are busy eradicating, the decadent obstructive, attitudes among the bourgeois elements of the civil service, last night we ask the technicians at TTT to broadcast a news conference of our primary aims an objectives, yer think dey do it, do it what, dey go an show a ole Wheel a Fortune episode, saying the tape get mix up, yer see what we have ter deal with, we don't have time to discuss your eating habits, eat cake

Lieutenants *rise in unison.*

Lieutenant le Grange Soldier, unlock the door,

Mikey *unlocks door.*

Lieutenant le Grange Take de chairs an table back to de Sergeant with our compliments, then lock de door, a know yer face, you was in my platoon for a while,

Mikey Yes, sir.

Lieutenant le Grange Yes, you was Corporal, an yer got busted down, a can't remember wat de offence was, well never mind, we in power now, is we country, don't forget that yer know,

Mikey No, sir,

Lieutenant le Grange We doing it fer the young proletarians like you, a too busy ter explain it now, but,

Mikey What, sir,

Lieutenant le Grange What, he want to know what, yer joking or what, is a coup, yer do' know what a coup is, yer do' know what's going on, yer been lock up in dis dungeon too long, man, all this, de revolution, it's liberation fer we, enjoy yerself, celebrate, but be vigilant, that's what going on, tell de people, an de masses, too,

Mikey Yes, sir,

Officers leave.

Mikey A have ter take dese out, sir,

President (*pacing with back to* **Mikey**) Why, no, that's not it, too sophisticated, no, maybe they simple enough to, no but,

Mikey *tries to take table and chairs in one trip, fails, leans rifle, takes table, returns, takes chairs, returns, takes rifle.*

Mikey A going ter lock up now, sir,

President Why,

Mikey A have ter sir,

President I mean why,

Mikey Sir,

President They need my confession, why, the scandal-mongers in town good enough to spread any story, apart from the

official news, I suppose it's all martial music, an pictures
of children picking hibiscus against a glorious sunrise, take
a seat, soldier,

Mikey *sits on bed*.

President You are about to be a vital part of your country's
history, you feel excited,

Mikey Yes, sir, my father tell me about,

President Forget what yer father tell yer, man, it's you, I'm
talking about, now, now is the time to make your mark, the
destiny of our country will be decided here,

Mikey How sir,

President You and me, soldier, we'll change it, together, they
need my signed confession, why, think, if they wanted to they
could have executed me, but they haven't, why,

Mikey I don't know notting bout dat, sir,

President Don't worry, think man, think, why, the people
already braying for my blood, why they need it,

Mikey I didn't hear notting bout braying, sir,

President Think soldier, put yourself in their place,

Mikey I can't do dat, sir,

President Alright, look, they have me, right, they have the
country, a curfew is in force, so why do they need a signed
confession from me, not just one, but a signed one,

Mikey So the people will believe what they say about you
is true,

President Bravo, well done, but not just our people, the
outside world, they going for aid, credit, money, soldier, they
trying to do a backdoor deal with America, I can't keep calling
you that, what is your name,

Mikey Michael, sir,

President I'll call you Mikey,

Mikey That's wat me friends call me,

President That's it, Mikey, recognition, they need recognition, the British an Americans haven't recognised them, they need my confession to sell them, but how much time we have, what other deals they doing, that's what we have to discover, but you have to play your part, as well,

Mikey Me, sir, I don't know notting bout dat, yer know, dat could get me in serious trouble,

President Yes, Mikey, but I am also asking you to save your country from a pack of wolves who will ravage it beyond recognition, I am asking you to be a small part of a process that restores the respect and dignity of independence to your country,

Mikey Boy, my father say you could talk,

President After that we'll let the people decide, what yer say,

Mikey I don't know, sir, I, don't,

President I know you don't want to get in trouble, all I want from you is information.

Mikey Wat kinda of information,

President I need to know what going on outside, the world reaction, what the rest of the Caribbean saying, have they recognised them, anything you can pick up, any news, so I can,

Mikey Wait, wait, sir, a sorry, I don't tink I can do dat, dat is serious charges, a 437 an a 734, facing me, right dey,

President I promise you won't,

Mikey (*gets up*) No, sir, I can't, I help you out wit the water an ting an talk to yer, but you talking firing squad der, if dey fine out, I can't tell you notting, I know Lieutenant le Grange, yer know, I serve under him, I had ter get thirty days ter get out from under him, he not easy,

President I give you my word, I wouldn't ask, (a) unless I thought you could do it, (b) you would not be caught, an it will be best, for our country,

Mikey No, sir, don't tell me an don't ask me notting, water dry up, (*Goes out, bangs door shut, locks it, walks off.*)

President (*shouts*) An I thought we had bred a generation of thoroughbreds, I never said it was going to be easy, (*Collapses on bed, to himself.*) I never said it was going to be,

Lights.

Scene Three

A beach. Sunset. A boat arrives, on board are European men: the **Captain** *of the ship,* **Christopher Columbus** *and a* **Monk**. *They disembark and the* **Captain** *plants the flag of Spain on top of a sandy hill.*

Columbus Padre,

Monk Gracious, my son, (*Crosses himself, kneels, holding crucifix, others kneel.*) *et domini patre et spirito santo*, oh holy father, once more by your almighty grace, we brave and humble sons of Spain, have travelled forth and find ourselves, on this far and distant shore, to proclaim to all, the majesty of your gospel and the divinity of your message,

Columbus Si, si, pronto,

Monk We pray that you,

Columbus Si, si,

Monk In the name of the Father the Son, the Holy Ghost, amen,

All rise, **Columbus** *grasps flag.*

Columbus In the name of their gracious majesties, King Ferdinand and Queen Isabella of Spain, and their holy empires, I name this island, whose three mountain peaks we sighted this daybreak, la Trinidad in remembrance of the Holy Trinity, I, hereby claim authority over all persons, lands, fisheries, livestock, grain, tar, precious metals and gem stones, on the island of Trinidad, God save the King, (*Others repeat.*) God save the Queen, (*Repeat.*) Amen, Captain, we will make camp here, it is here, it must be here,

Captain Si, conquistador, it will be as you say, (*Goes.*)

Columbus What you say Padre, it is here Padre, it must be here, we have searched everywhere, it must be,

Monk Observe the birds, señor, have you ever seen such plumage, before,

Columbus (*taking telescope*) Where, where,

Monk There señor, in the trees,

Columbus Which, where, where, that one, where,

Monk There señor, that one, with the beautiful golden fruit, there señor, the birds are eating the fruit, they eat the fruit, with hands they eat the fruit, señor, they are not birds, señor, they are people, señor, natives,

Columbus Capitan,

Captain Si, señor,

Columbus Signal the ships, to prepare cannons,

Captain Si, señor,

Columbus Tell them if they see a red flag, they are to fire, a white they are to hold,

Captain Si, señor,

Columbus Then deploy your men, to a defensive position,

Captain Si, señor,

Captain *goes*.

Monk Such colours, such strength, to climb so high, observe the height of the tree, the thinnest of its branches, how do they arrive, there,

Columbus Fool Padre, what you say, you say they fly,

Monk Forgive me your grace, but I cannot help what I see before me, branches, so thin, birds so many, and so large, see, one is arriving señor, madre, it is a miracle, señor, he can, they are man, man can fly, señor, do you understand what we have discovered, do you, (*Kneels.*)

Columbus Fool Padre, (*Takes telescope, kicks* **Monk**.) first it's a bird, then it's a man, now it's a miracle, get up Padre, I tell you this, man does not fly and birds do not eat fruit with hands,

Monk Señor, they have seen us, they are coming towards us, Santa Maria,

Columbus Take hold of yourself, Padre, Capitán, alert the Santa Maria,

Dark shadows cover the camp. The Arawaks arrive, dressed in feathers of gold, golden jewellery, carrying baskets of fruit.

Columbus (*to* **Native Priest**) In the name of their holy majesties King Ferdinand and Queen Isabella of Spain, I Christopher Columbus, claim dominion over this land, inhabitants and possessions, in return we grant, the protection of their sovereign majesties and the blessings, of our Holy Father, Jesus Christ,

Priest (*offers fruit*) Eat, eat,

Columbus Speak to him Padre,

Monk (*crosses*) *In nomine patris et filii et spiritu sancti*, children, how, in the name of the holy spirit, how do you fly, how can you,

Priest Eat, eat,

Columbus (*grabs necklace*) This, this, gold, where do you find it, this gold,

Monk *picks up fruit, eats.*

Priest El Dorado, El Dorado, very far away, a city, a golden city, where the streets are paved with golden pebbles, where golden natives blow golden horns, in golden temples, where golden moisture slowly drips, from golden windows, and golden virgins dance in golden veils, to golden melodies played, on golden harps, to the lash of golden whips, where golden horses' golden droppings, make the golden soil to grow this golden fruit, so eat, eat,

Columbus Yes, yes, I was right, my dream was right, Padre, a golden city, you, you must take us there, you must take me, I must see it, before I,

Priest Then eat, and we will fly there,

Columbus But that's not possible, man does not fly,

Priest That is the only way he can see it,

Columbus But he cannot, man cannot fly, he can think, he can act, but he, (*Picks up red flag.*) See, a red flag can fly, but not man, he cannot fly,

Priest Then he must, die,

Cannons open fire, camp site is hit, natives rise off.

Scene Four

The cell. **President** *asleep on bed.*

President No, no, he can, he can,

Mikey (*shaking man*) Yer alright sir, sir, yer alright,

President Who, no, no, don't, what,

Mikey Yer was talking sir, in yer sleep, yer was,

President What, yes, yes, thank you,

Mikey *goes out, locks door.*

President Thanks, (*Beat.*) I'm glad you're back,

Mikey I'm on duty sir, we still on orders,

President Yes, yes, I would like that drink a water now,

Mikey Yes, sir, (*Goes.*)

President *looks at wrist, gets up, staggers, sits on bed,* **Mikey** *returns, unlocks door brings in water.*

President Thank you, I,

Mikey Here, an piece a bread an butter,

President What about news, yer have any news,

Mikey You really want to see me in trouble, don't yer, alright, yer wife an family down at a officers' quarters, down at Tetron Bay, sir, under heavy guard, yer satisfied,

President Yes, thank you, what else, any,

Mikey Yes, the Committee turn Governor House into a sports headquarters, an the ballroom into a indoor basketball court, with the hoops hanging from the chandeliers, but the hoops en have no nets an the national team say they not practising with no nets, because the nets have a certain way of helping the ball in, an they been working that move, an when they come to play a international game they'll be out of touch, the nets tied up on the docks because of the dock strike, because the stevedores say they not moving East German goods, so all the people in the mad house weaving baskets outa fine straw twine, yer could beat dat?

President Yes, yes, that's good, but what about the outside world, England, America, what they saying,

Mikey I didn't hear notting bout them, sir, but a feller say the United Nations, waiting on you to make a protest,

President That's not true, they know, (*Beat.*) they must know, they wouldn't let me down, (*Beat.*) I know, they waiting, what the papers saying,

Mikey What papers, the Committee take over the papers an only printing sports stories, bout Kenny Rampersad going for his double century on a turning pitch, his hobbies include horse riding, among other things,

President Like what,

Mikey Scuba diving,

President What about the situation,

Mikey Things about you, sir,

President Yes, like what, tell me,

Mikey Stories, like,

President I know they're lies,

Mikey That you give the helicopter contract to the French DSCV company in return for seven diamonds that the late African Emperor Bokassa gave them, in return for the special refrigerators they made for him, to keep human flesh fresh, things like that, an how you have a mistress in Miami called Monique Montaine, an she station a photographer outside her motel window and pay a big pimp to burst in on you an she jamming in the nude an she using the photographs to blackmail you for fifty thousand dollars a year to supply her an her pimp with cocaine, alongside with pictures of schools, water pumps, tractors, two seed machines an a electric plough from Rumania, an saying fifty thousand dollars a year would buy all that for de people,

President An the television,

Mikey The usual stories,

President Same kinda thing,

Mikey Yes, sir, even in your day, you never printed dem kinda tings,

President Thank you, Corporal, you see I was right, that's why, that's why we have to have a plan, a purpose, we,

Mikey Hold on, I do' know notting bout no plan or purpose, yer know, an who is this we, I help you enough I going to help you, sir, you ask me fer water, I give you water, you ask me for news, I give you news, I give you more than news, an what's all this Corporal business,

President Don't you see, we have to stop them, an you're pardoned of all charges, what's the time, they took my watch,

Mikey (*shouts*) I not suppose to tell you that, yer know (*Shows him wristwatch.*)

President How come a ex-Corporal can afford a Boluva watch,

Mikey Sir, even in your day, de regiment was in business, yer know,

President So,

Mikey Alright, alright, what yer want, yer see you,

President We need to contact America and England, we need to know what they doing, what they planning, we need,

Mikey Wait, wait a minute, what you saying, wat is this contact business,

President You or somebody have to contact them,

Mikey An how we go do dat, with submarine,

President Somebody have to go to the Embassy or the High Commission,

Mikey Stop, just stop, right there, contact, you, somebody, somebody, you, I know wat you was getting at, somebody,

you mean me, don't you, there's nobody else an I en sending
my woman, so is me you mean,

President If I could I would,

Mikey Look sir, forget it, you don't know wat you talking
bout, in the first place, A an B company have all the embassies
ringed with APC's with HMG's mounted on sandbags, for
their protection from the angry proletariat, in the second
place, the ladies netball team turn up to collect their visas
an A company panic an taught they were a rapid react strike
force an shoot the coach in the leg, an you asking me, wat
a saying, you asking somebody, not somebody me, to stroll
up dey an say wha happen dey fellers, an, forget it, you,
you, sir,

President Yer don't see, the stevedores on strike, that's a
good sign, now the netball team on strike, that's another
good sign, they don't have the people, we need to know
what de Americans thinking, then we'll stop them, an army
can only win with good intelligence,

Mikey Wat army, wat you coming with now,

President Us, you an me, we are the army, we are the army
that will defeat them, you know the boys in A company, you
could do it, I,

Mikey I know, you can't,

President At the Embassy, say, you want to speak to Mister
Roberts about some books, at the High Commission ask for
Mister Creighton, tell him, you have a message from your
President, tell him,

Mikey No, I en telling nobody nothing, no way, that's it,
you get water an news, because a feel sorry for you, dats
all, notting else, yer hear, not me, I en marching up an
saluting in front no firing squad, not even to save me own
mother,

President What about yer country,

Mikey What, yer see you, yer know someting sir, a was right, a was going to say it an a hold me tongue, but, sir or no sir, you mad, sir, yer hear, yer finish with the water, (*Takes cup, goes out, locks door.*) mad, (*Beat.*) mad,

President I'd just like to say, how grateful I am, for what you've done so far, and when the time comes,

Mikey Go away,

President It seemed like a good idea at the time, (*Beat.*) it was worth a try, (*Beat.*) much better than the one of curfews, street searches, late night pick-ups, bloated bodies floating in Caroni swamps, the corbeaux will think this island is a banquet, no fêtes, no carnival,

Mikey They'd never do dat, de people would never stand fer it, (*Beat.*) Never, (*Beat.*) never, not in a million years, you really think they'd do dat, (*Beat.*) dem things,

President Not they, you, you'll be doing it, they'll give the orders, an drive off in their Zod limousines to Mirama Night club, they had brothels in East Germany, you know, reserved for visiting heads of state,

Mikey I didn't know that, (*Beat.*)

President That's the truth, an they're very efficient, well trained,

Mikey Yes, yer tried it eh,

President I'm a Trinidadian man, apart from bad manners, it would have been very bad taste to say no to Helga, when I was looking after the Trade Ministry, I went to Leipzig to negotiate a flour deal, you remember the shortage we had in '51.

Mikey No,

President No, well you wouldn't, because there wasn't one, Helga an I averted that one, at reasonable terms, all parties were satisfied by the outcome,

Mikey (*laughs*) After all, you had to keep up de Trini name,

President Yes, she was a beauty, I asked her, you know, if she'd like to come an live in the West, I could have arranged it, it would have cost us a few bulldozers, but it would have been good value, (*Beat.*)

Mikey She was that juicy, eh,

President Black hair, blue eyes and a mole right here (*Goes to grill, points to face, next to lips.*) an when she smiled it moved upwards, an freckles, freckles everywhere, she was a country girl, but what a woman, yes, she would have been worth it,

Mikey An wat happened,

President She said, she liked it there, she liked the life, she didn't want to leave,

Mikey It wasn't such a bad idea, yer know,

President Yes, which one,

Mikey Yer like a lot of ideas, don't you,

President Never trust a socialist, now, who said that, was it Churchill or Harold Wilson, you know when Wilson invaded Anguilla, I said to him, Harold how could you as a socialist do a thing like that, boy the ole chimney came out, an all a could hear coming from the maze of smoke, was British interest was at stake, British interest, for the life of me, I,

Mikey It was you sir,

President Me,

Mikey Yes, yer said it at a passing out parade at Chagaramus Barracks when yer was coming up fer re-election, an there was de scandal about the telephones contract going to de French at de time, an I had to listen to every word yer say, because I was first to step forward to receive the silver baton, as top recruit in my company,

President An I presented it to you,

Mikey Yes, sir,

President That was good,

Mikey Yes, sir,

President Right, this is what we have to do.

Shout from corridor.

Black Lightning Attention, down there, officers approaching,

Mikey *stands to attention. Calls coming down line, three guards.*

Major Ferret Sentries on duty,

Guard 1 Sentry on duty, sir,

Major Ferret Sentries on duty,

Guard 2 Sentry on duty, sir,

Major Ferret Sentries on duty,

Guard 3 Sentry on duty, sir,

Major Ferret Sentries on duty,

Mikey Sentry on duty sir,

Major Ferret Yer have keys,

Mikey Yes sir,

Major Ferret Right open de door, den take a walk,

Soldier *opens door, walks.*

Major Ferret Wait, wait,

Mikey Sir,

Major Ferret Go an get a table an two chairs,

Mikey Yes, sir, (*Goes.*)

Major Ferret *enters cell, accompanied by a sergeant,* **Black Lightning**. **Major Ferret** *is thirty-ish, a light skinned Trinidadian*

of mixed parentage. **Black Lightning** *is of African origin. Also, thirty-ish.*

Major Ferret Mister President, I am Major Ferret, (*Goes, offers hand to* **President, President** *does not.*)

President Yes, we've met, I didn't know you was part of this, I thought at least a man of your experience, would respect your oath to your country, and the tradition of your profession, but that's another story,

Major Ferret Mister President, there comes a time when the forces of history are so strong that tradition and respect have to take second place to the greater good of your people as you see it, and you either go along with those forces or be swept aside, by them, but I didn't come here to argue the intricacies of Freudian politics with you, I have here,

Takes confession out of briefcase, **Mikey** *enters with table,* **Major Ferret** *puts confession on table, takes biro out of pocket, uncaps it,* **Mikey** *goes.*

Major Ferret A confession a want you to sign, now there's two ways we can do this, de easy way, or de hard way, now let me tell you bout de easy way, yer see de easy way goes like dis, you pick up de pen, an yer move yer hand over ter dat line, no, sorry, that one there an yer sign yer name, easy, a sure yer have de energy to do dat, all dat exercising yer do in Miami yer must be fit, dat's de easy way, now let me tell yer bout de hard way, yer see a just wince, that's because I don't even like talking bout de hard way, it does make me pores raise an de hairs on me hands stand up, yer know wat a mean, an why yer tink dat is, a go tell yer, it's because I see de hard way in action an believe me it's not nice, an is all down to de Sergeant here, he don't like nobody, not even me, right Sergeant,

Black Lightning Sir,

Major Ferret What's dat, Sergeant a didn't hear yer,

Black Lightning Yes, sir,

Major Ferret A still didn't hear yer, yer have ter speak louder dan dat yer know, it's not me but de President here might be hard of hearing, it comes with age, so let's hear yer,

Black Lightning (*shouts*) Yes, sir,

Major Ferret Ahh, dat's better, did you hear dat, did you hear dat sir,

President Yes I heard it, I heard a frightened soldier obeying a frightening officer,

Major Ferret Oh, yer notice dat too eh, because dat save me de trouble of having to tell you why de Sergeant frightened because he know dat if he is de meanest, I am de meanest meanest, yer saw dat eh, I didn't think yer would, I've been underrating you all this time, man, a have to revise my facts, what yer say Sergeant,

Black Lightning (*shouts*) Yes, sir,

Major Ferret Yer don't have ter shout Sergeant, a tink de President's hearing is in working order, now,

Mikey *enters with chairs.*

Major Ferret Where yer went, ter de lumber yard ter get dem,

Mikey No sir,

Major Ferret Alright, alright, da was a joke, go on, yes, where a was,

President You were telling me, about the hard way,

Major Ferret Oh, yes, the hard way, yer see how I don't like talking bout it, yes, I thought we had finish with dat, yer see, I does get carried away an sidetracked, yes, de hard way, (*Laughs.*) yer want ter hear someting really funny sir,

President Yes, they say, laughter has a civilising influence,

Major Ferret Oh, yes, yes, then you'll like this, you're a civilised man, so civilised, mothers have ter wrap up de new born babies in de hospital because de maternity ward run out a linen, whilst you take off in yer BWIA jet to visit yer woman in Miami, man you civilised for so, what yer say, Sergeant, yer could shout dis time,

Black Lightning (*shouts*) Yes, sir,

Major Ferret Yer see, even de Sergeant agree yer civilised, but a getting carried away again, yer see, a tell a have ter watch me self, dey go lock me up in St Ann's next, oh, by the way, dat was a good move yer made,

President What was dat,

Major Ferret Getting de Americans to pay fer de new shock treatment system at de madhouse,

President You know those are lies,

Major Ferret Yes, well as I said, I didn't come here to argue politics, but yes, back ter de hard way, but wait a was going ter give yer a joke, let me see if a remember, no don't help me, a was going to tell yer a joke, den a got carried away by yer civilising influence ting, yes, de joke is, is all down ter you an de Americans, yer see dat exchange scheme you an de Americans work out when yer went ter Miami, dat dey would send down some instructors from Fort Bragg, well dat's when I first saw de potential, of the hard way, a glimpse, a vision of the man in action, you'll appreciate dis, being a civilised man, see if yer could visualise it, the grace of Comrade Nijinsky, the strength of Comrade Nureyev, an the zen of Bruce Lee, all rolled into one, poetry in motion, man, a killing machine, it's the hands, yer just don't know where dey coming from, dat combined with a basic knowledge of de human anatomy, it's lethal, a hope yer getting some idea a what a driving at yer know because, I find is always better when people understand each other, tings seem to go better, yer know what a mean, an we don't have all night, my wife have dinner waiting fer me an ternight is dumpling an saltfish an if you know how much I like dumpling an saltfish, you'd understand what a telling yer,

President I understand,

Major Ferret That's good, because, tings just go better dat way, right, Sergeant an yer don't have ter shout dis time,

Black Lightning Right, sir,

Major Ferret Yer see, even de Sergeant understand, too, so what's it to be, yer go make my wife happy, an let me get home in time ter enjoy my saltfish an dumplings hot, an de Sergeant watch de East European quarter finals, from Bucharest, or yer get ter reap de rewards of yer hard negotiations in Miami, she could always reheat it, what de heck, is de salvation of our people we dealing with, so yer see either way we en leaving here without yer confession signed, what yer say, pretend yer signing a cheque for another fur coat for yer lady wife,

President Major Ferret or John Wayne, or whatever you call yourself, since you have seen it fit to deprive me of the basic necessities of human nourishment, I will make this short, I will tell you exactly what I told your brother officers, I have no intention of justifing your cowboy fantasies, to wreak even more havoc on the lives of the good people of Trinidad an Tobago, as your lawfully elected President an Commander in Chief, I command you release all elected members of your government, my wife and family from Tetron Bay, return to barracks at Chagaramas where you will place yourselves under arrest, then I give you my word as President, you will be given an opportunity to state your case before the courts, an a jury of your much loved countrymen, now if there is nothing else, I would like to get some rest, (*Lies on bed.*)

Major Ferret What happen ter dis man, or what, he don't hear, I get de Sergeant ter shout till he hoarse an yer still don't get de message, what yer say Sergeant, didn't you shout till yer hoarse,

Black Lightning (*quietly*) Sir,

Major Ferret Yer see, yer upsetting de Sergeant now, sign de ting man, I for one don't want him to get too upset, den he might forget heself an, but, yer en even read it, how you could say yer en signing someting an yer en read it, you might even like it, all it say is, (*Picks up paper.*) right, you sorry for

de crimes you committed against de people of Trinidad an
Tobago, an yer could go, you, yer family, we have a armed
escort for yer own protection, waiting to take you to a glorious
exile, somewhere,

President Major, de day I need protection from de people
of Trinidad an Tobago, I will save you an your Sergeant de
trouble an do the job myself, end of story, now good night,
an don't forget to close the door behind you,

Major Ferret An rob me of de pleasure of seeing a real artist
at work, yer see wat a always tell yer Sergeant nothing in life
is wasted, as well as a signed confession tonight we getting a
lesson in pre-colonial manners, but wait, how you know yer
family down at Tetron, you not suppose to know dat, a, a,
dat's de second time yer surprise me, what a pity you couldn't
see de dynamic forces of change coming at yer, when you refuse
to let de Cuban literacy teachers come here dat was yer last
mistake,

President They could only teach Spanish, they were highly
trained organising commissars,

Major Ferret Who told yer, was it Lieutenant Chan, or le
Grange,

President Who told me what,

Major Ferret Dat yer family was down at Tetron, under
guard,

President No one told me, I assumed that's where you would
take them, to be secure,

Major Ferret Was it Lieutenant Chan,

President No, no one,

Major Ferret Le Grange den,

President No, no one,

Major Ferret Someting's not right here, yer know, tings going
according to plan, an suddenly outa de blue, you know your

family at Tetron, I don't work so, steelband iron start ringing in my ears, an I have to say to myself, do I believe dis man so smart dat he telling de truth, or someone or somebody tell him an he covering up something with dis someone or somebody, an (*Beat.*) so if it wasn't Lieutenant Chan or le Grange dere's only one other little birdy left, wat yer say Sergeant, yer getting de picture,

Black Lightning Yes, sir,

Major Ferret Thank you Sergeant, (*Beat.*) Mister President are you still with us, (*Beat.*) Sergeant wake de President,

President I'm awake,

Major Ferret Good then, Sergeant be a pussy cat an go an catch de little birdy,

President (*gets up*) No, wait, it was Chan, Chan, an le Grange, Chan said it but le Grange was there,

Major Ferret Ahhhhha I knew it, Chan, an le Grange, le Grange an Chan, right,

President Yes,

Major Ferret Right, you witnessing dis Sergeant,

Black Lightning Yes, sir,

Major Ferret So is Chan an le Grange who's been leaking tings to de reactionaries, right, so wat else, wat else dey tell you, dey tell yer dis confession ting is dere idea an de Sergeant here an I would just like to blow yer away, well dey was right, but now is dem go feel de breeze, yer hear dat Sergeant,

Black Lightning Yes, sir,

Major Ferret Wat else dey ask yer ter sign, dey ask yer ter sign any cheques or anyting like dat, or how to move currency before a devaluation of de dollar,

President No, so even de poor dollar getting it too,

Major Ferret De IMF suspend we loan an demanding de back interest, de money you an yer cronies squandered on sweet living, but dem days, finish with, dat's someting, you an de Chans an de le Granges of dis world don't understand, but alyer go find out, Sergeant, ask the President what else, what other piece of paper Lieutenants Chan an le Grange asked him to sign, or asked him to read,

Black Lightning Yes, sir,

Major Ferret What other, (*Moves towards* **President**.)

President No wait,

Major Ferret Ahh, Trinidadian common sense of survival, prevails, yes, wat was it, wat was it he wanted yer to sign, a amnesty, for him, him an le Grange in case de mutiny fail, is dat it, eh, wat you tink Sergeant, yer tink dat's it, de lottery an daily double, an dat big bottom whore from Abercromby Street all rolled into one, wat yer say,

Black Lightning It sound so to me sir,

Major Ferret Thank you Sergeant, well Sergeant it look like we have we work cut out fer we, wat yer say we wrap dis one up an go an fry some other fish, Sergeant ask de President if Lieutenants Chan an le Grange ask him ter sign any amnesties for dem or any other officers,

Black Lightning Yes, sir, (*Moves towards* **President**.)

President No, wait, yes, yes, yes, they did, they did, they didn't ask me to sign one, they just showed me a first draft of one, an I made certain suggestions an they agreed to return with an amended version,

Major Ferret What were their conditions,

President Impossible,

Major Ferret No, what dey was asking for, full court martial with full reinstatement of rank an pensions, all civil charges dropped, something like dat,

President Something like that, why should I help you topple your brother officers, so you can inflict your brand of suffering on the people,

Major Ferret Right we get what we want, Sergeant show de President who is boss,

Black Lightning You mean hit im,

Major Ferret No, I mean break his neck, slowly,

Black Lightning Why, sir,

Major Ferret That was an order, Sergeant,

Black Lightning But sir, you always say a good soldier always should question a order but obey it, that by questioning something we discover de underlying meanings an levels of perceptions behind it, dat's what I'm doing now, sir, an I car discover no meanings or perceptions, a know you like ter see me in action an ting, but I don't really like hurting people yer know, not really, a enjoy de skill, but not de pain,

President Sergeant, you should take up golf,

Black Lightning Yer tink so sir,

President Yes, very relaxing, especially if you have a bad back,

Black Lightning I does have some back trouble, usually in the shoulders here, yer feel dat, a tink a get it from the body slam, maybe a should shift me weight over to me right shoulder, when a, yer see sir, de only levels of perception I getting is dat, with Lieutenant Chan an le Grange running bout waving amnesty paper, an de whores stop giving we credit, blaming we because they en have no food in de shops, fight breaking out all over de place because people going into shops talking Yankee an saying dey is part of a liberating force an getting credit on household appliances, you always tell me a successful revolution have to win de hearts an minds of de people, like a fish in a large sea, but nobody know wat going on, I confused, you tell me get rid a dis one, Lieutenant Chan an le Grange say get rid a dat one, I en complaining yer know, but I could end up having ter take de rap for everyting,

Major Ferret But you have no cause to fear, the revolution is strong, for every movement there is an equal an opposite reaction, we just have to apply a equally harder reaction an wipe dem out, is I commanding the revolution now, yer know,

Black Lightning Yes, sir, I en saying dat, sir, all I saying is tings looking confusing and dat, say, in case, just in case, I en saying it go happen you know, but suppose, just suppose de people change dey mind an decide dey do like wat we doing an want ter go back ter de ole days, somebody go have ter take de rap for all dis, an it go be me,

Major Ferret You were obeying orders,

Black Lightning Yes, sir, but de trouble with dat is, dey don't catch de man who give de order because he might have a amnesty paper in he top pocket too, an you ferget something else, sir, I don't like doing it,

President Well done, Sergeant, spoken like a true Trini,

Black Lightning Thank you, sir,

Major Ferret Alright Sergeant, a didn't mean it, just testing, a was just waiting to see if you had perceived the long term ramifications of removing the President now, or for long term purposes maintaining the symbolism of the office, an a must say, back there a had me doubts, but yer come through, yer come through with flying colours, well done,

Black Lightning Thank you, sir,

Major Ferret No, once more I find myself in admiration of you, a big fish deserves a big fisherman, I must be more aware of my sense of history, this is our national saviour, we taking out, the man who lead we into independence an kept us in bondage ever since, Sergeant, give me your pistol,

Black Lightning Yes, sir,

Hands it over, **Major Ferret** *pulls bolt.*

Major Ferret Mister President, do you have any famous last words for students of contemporary Caribbean politics,

President Yes, what about the Sergeant, are you going to kill him too,

Major Ferret Very good, civilised to the last, the Sergeant is a student of life, he understands, nothing stands in the way of a movement whose time has arrived, (*Aims.*) Mister President, on behalf of the people of Trinidad an Tobago, I hereby execute you, power to the people,

Lights go out, shots are fired, **Major Ferret** *shouts in pain, a beat.*

Black Lightning Sir, yer dead, yer alright,

Major Ferret Shh, where you,

Black Lightning Over here,

Major Ferret A tink yer better come over here, Fort Bragg style,

Black Lightning Yer sure, sir,

Major Ferret Yes, man that's an order, crawl over here,

Black Lightning Why, sir,

Major Ferret A bleeding man, a tink a get hit, a think one a de 9mm short impact head, ricochet off the wall an hit me,

Black Lightning A coming, (*Crawls over to* **Major Ferret**.) a here sir, where yer, yer soaking, sir,

Major Ferret Yes, you have to get me out of here,

Black Lightning How, sir,

Major Ferret You have to carry me,

Black Lightning I can't do dat sir, me shoulder,

Major Ferret Alright, drag me out by the shoulders, Swiss army style,

Black Lightning Alright sir,

Begins to slowly drag **Major Ferret** *out*.

Major Ferret Yer think we get him,

Black Lightning Yes, sir, he quiet, (*Going out.*)

Major Ferret Why, why, yer take so long to come over an help, me, man,

Black Lightning Sir, a tell yer someting funny, I thought you was going to take me out, too, (*Laughs.*)

Major Ferret (*laughs*) Me, not me man, I wouldn't dream of doing something like that,

Lights. Sound of gunfire, explosions, in distance.

Scene Five

The cell, **President** *is lying on floor. Lights,* **Mikey** *enters, goes to* **President**.

Mikey Oh, God, sir, yer alright,

President Yes, yes, I'm alright, what happen, give me a hand,

Mikey *helps* **President** *up over to bed*.

Mikey Call it a miracle, sir, I was outside in de corridor playing heads I win tails you lose with Corporal Jadoo, an as I jump up to catch de twenty-five cent piece, he does cheat yer see, I hear Major Ferret say power to de people an I hook de sling on my SLR on de fuse-box handle, an blackout, it look like Major Ferret get hit, I help put him in de back of de APC an they gone out de gates, with anti-personnel sirens blaring,

President (*laughs*) It was indeed a miracle, it's called being born a Trinidadian, consider yourself acting, no, no, full Sergeant, now,

Mikey Thank you, sir,

President So Ferret shoot himself, serve him right, a bet yer it won't be the last, de fool can't even shoot straight, (*Laughs.*) well, de Republic's luck still holding, thanks to,

Mikey Sir, yer get a graze,

President (*searching head*) Where,

Mikey There, (*Forehead.*)

President Yes, so a did,

Mikey I'll go an get de first aid kit,

President No, no, forget about that, we don't have time, we have work to do,

Mikey I'd like to sir, it don't look right we President with blood on his head,

President Alright, but hurry up,

Mikey Yes, sir,

Goes on double, returns, dresses wound.

President Well boy, we really have dem on de run, now, yer get ter de Embassy,

Mikey Take it easy sir, yer lose some blood,

President What's a little blood for the Republic eh, like we first meetings, de opposition used ter hire de best stone pelters in de district ter terrorise we, but we learn ter duck, so what, yer going or not,

Mikey Keep still sir, I don't know,

President Yer still fraid,

Mikey Yes, of course a fraid, but,

President We have to, yer don't see we an de people have dem going round in circles, we winning, all we need is de Americans to know that, an ter hold delay recognition an we back in business,

Mikey Yer sure about that,

President Yes,

Mikey An dat's all,

President I give you my word,

Mikey An notting else, (*Beat.*) well, wen I was down by de guard hut, a was talking ter de boys, an dey getting fed up with de officers too,

President Yer see, we,

Mikey Hold on, hold on, if we doing this we have to do it right, yer know, we car go stirring up nothing if we don't know what it is,

President Right,

Mikey So you say, if we get a message ter dis, Mister Creighton, at de Embassy, then,

President No, Creighton at de commission, Roberts at de Embassy,

Mikey Right, Roberts at de Embassy, Creighton at de commission,

President Right,

Mikey Well, dat en no problem, yer see, because de boys tell me dey only letting in de cleaning girls in de Embassy because, de NCO's wife have de cleaning franchise, an,

President Yes,

Mikey An my woman does clean fer she,

President Wonderful, (*Embraces* **Mikey**.)

Mikey Take it easy ner, so,

President So all you have ter do is give her de message,

Mikey Right, yer catch on fast,

President Just trying to keep up,

Mikey Well, keep up faster, sir, de Major boasting an telling everybody you dead, so you stay dead, right, believe me it safer, until we can sneak you out an den, well, de rest is up to you, so get some now,

President What,

Mikey Rest,

President Yes, I'm a bit shaky now, an thank you, for everything, (*Lies down.*)

Mikey (*tucks him in*) You lie down sir,

President What about yer woman, (*Half rises.*)

Mikey Relax sir, she passing later, before she go to work,

Shout from down corridor.

Black Lightning Attention, down there, officers approaching,

President *covers head with white sheet.*

Lieutenant Chan Sentries on duty,

Mikey Sentry on duty sir,

Lieutenant le Grange Sentries on duty,

Enter **Lieutenants Chan** *and* **Le Grange**, *they slowly, go over to body pistols drawn.* **Mikey** *at attention.*

Lieutenant Chan Soldier, what going on here,

Mikey President Jones dead, sir, Major Ferret was here an dere was a accident an some shooting an,

Lieutenant Chan Dat maniac, yer see wha a tell yer, a knew it, boy, yer see dat man, I always say Ferret was unstable, an now he prove it,

Lieutenant le Grange But how he could go do a thing like this, at this critical stage of the revolution man, the committee voted to threaten, just threaten, nobody vote for killing, you vote fer any killing,

Lieutenant Chan No, he gone power mad, man,

Lieutenant le Grange The man betraying all the ideals of the revolution, just wen we trying to get the people to respect we, he go an do a ting like this, we in real trouble now, dere's no way we can camouflage this, de President, ter shoot de President just like that, man, you is my witness, we never approved this,

Lieutenant Chan We have ter keep we heads, man, this situation calls for some serious reasoning, alright, soldier take a walk,

Mikey *goes.*

Yer notice he didn't salute,

Lieutenant le Grange You worrying bout that man, this whole thing could blow up an backfire in we face, an you, is we blood dey go be coming for, not that little disobedience campaign going on now, boy, that man, is, is, as if, he, he, like, a, a, I don't like how this beginning to look you know, it beginning to look like set up, man, I smell set up here, Ferret set we up, he do it deliberate, he know what go happen when de news burst, boy, I smell a rat here, a big rat, an it spell with three letters too, C-I-A, a bet yer two ter one, right now, he cook up a deal with Larry Roberts to stick we with this an come out looking, Mister Clean, neat eh,

Lieutenant Chan Ferret, CIA, yer tink so,

Lieutenant le Grange Yer don't see, de black market giving out ration cards, everything about to blow, then de master touch, de deposed Head of State is assassinated, classic, classic CIA scenario, man, de perfect excuse to invade an set up Ferret with a right wing government, yer see what happen wen yer try ter be too democratic,

Lieutenant Chan An you think Ferret set it up,

Lieutenant le Grange He more than set it up, man, he design an construct it,

Lieutenant Chan Yer tink so,

Lieutenant le Grange A know it,

Lieutenant Chan A mean, yer really tink so,

Lieutenant le Grange A tell yer, a know de beast, de,

Lieutenant Chan You really tink Ferret so, so, devious ter do a thing like dat,

Lieutenant le Grange Yes, an I'll tell yer something else, a bet yer we names is next, on he hit parade, the man stick we, all ways,

Lieutenant Chan Yer tink so,

Lieutenant le Grange What yer keep asking me dat for, of course a tink so, a wouldn't say so if a didn't think so, wouldn't you,

Lieutenant Chan I,

Lieutenant le Grange Right, we have ter read dis situation right yer know, or we is history, too,

Lieutenant Chan Boy, dat man is a real heavyweight, a have ter hand it ter him yes, yes, yer right, what we do,

Lieutenant le Grange We have ter highjack this ting man, before it highjack we,

Lieutenant Chan How we go do that,

Lieutenant le Grange Alright, let we look at we options,

Lieutenant Chan Alright, but let we do it somewhere else, I can't handle dead bodies, man,

Lieutenant le Grange This place safe man, alright, we have to plan some moves, I say, we go an pick up we men, take de body to Television House, (*Checks time.*) interrupt de boxing finals, with Beethoven number five, show de people de body of dere beloved President, dey bound to feel sorry for we,

Lieutenant Chan Then what,

Lieutenant le Grange Then we announce another coup, with some heavy steelband music in de background, make de people feel good one time, we proclaim in de name of the people love of democracy, the overthrow of the corrupt and immoral regime of Major Ferret, by a group of young patriotic officers, who, when they came to rescue the President, found his body, dead,

Lieutenant Chan Who's dat,

Lieutenant le Grange We who, when they came to rescue the President, found his body dead,

Lieutenant Chan Right, then what,

Lieutenant le Grange Then we declare a state of national mourning, people go party till they fall, then we move on Government House an waste Ferret, and, a buzzing, a buzzing, and, as well as de body, we mention de discovery of the remains of human flesh in the seven refrigerators, along with certain black magic instruments, we found in his private apartment with two-way, gold mirrors on de walls, plus the disappearance of two million Deutschmarks earmarked for the national netball stadium, missing from the National Bank,

Lieutenant Chan He take dat much,

Lieutenant le Grange Dat's how much he going to take, one fer you, one fer me,

Lieutenant Chan Oh, right, right, boy you smart, then what,

Lieutenant le Grange You asking me, you always asking me, then what, as if we playing some follow my leader, it's equal rank equal responsibility, man, what they teach yer at Sandhurst,

Lieutenant Chan Assess your position, an determine if you can hold or,

Lieutenant le Grange In other words, watch yer ass, right,

Lieutenant Chan Right, what about the Americans,

Lieutenant le Grange Dey en go be no problem man, is their man Ferret freak out on some LSD they try out on him, an waste de President, so dey can't make a sound, then we convince dem we straight,

Lieutenant Chan How we do that,

Lieutenant le Grange We,

President Release all political prisioners,

Lieutenant Chan That's smart,

Lieutenant le Grange What's smart, a know what de other smarts for, but what was de last one for,

Lieutenant Chan What yer just said,

Lieutenant le Grange What I just say,

Lieutenant Chan Yer just said, we release all political prisoners, something along the lines I was,

Lieutenant le Grange I didn't say that, you did, I said we have ter convince them, yer hearing tings, or what, but a see what yer mean, certain political prisoners, that's good, what's the big thing dey hassling us for,

Lieutenant Chan Reopening de Coca Cola factory,

Lieutenant le Grange No, man, de biggy,

Lieutenant Chan De Amarco assets we nationalise,

Lieutenant le Grange No, man, yer give up, restoration of the presidency, we find ex-Vice President, Charles, he was always backstabbing for the job anyway,

Lieutenant Chan If he still alive, (*Laughing.*)

Lieutenant le Grange If he still alive, a President io a President is a President, right, in return, Prime Minister an Ministry of Defence for me an National Security an Finance for you, nobody breathes, unless we say so, what yer think, not bad, eh,

Lieutenant Chan Smart, I think it's smart, like all your moves, man, smart,

Lieutenant le Grange Den we say to them, we prepared to consider certain steps for the restoration of democracy, starting with a massive IMF loan, full resumption of military aid,

Lieutenant Chan A visit by de Harlem Globetrotters,

Lieutenant le Grange What dey have ter do with dis,

Lieutenant Chan A like dem, man,

Lieutenant le Grange Alright, a visit from de Globetrotters, an freedom from any congressional hearings,

Lieutenant Chan Alright, why yer didn't say dat in de first place, all dat shit bout voices, what else,

President Free an open elections,

Lieutenant le Grange No man,

Lieutenant Chan No what,

Lieutenant le Grange No free an open elections,

Lieutenant Chan Who say, dat,

Lieutenant le Grange You did,

Lieutenant Chan I didn't say, you did, who hearing voices now,

Lieutenant le Grange I wouldn't say that, man, I know I wouldn't say dat, no, no free an open elections,

Lieutenant Chan I thought we was supposed to be discussing this, equally,

Lieutenant le Grange Alright, but we declare a one party state, yer mustn't take everything so literally, man, yer must be more pragmatic,

Lieutenant Chan Alright, don't get vex, ner, it's de body man,

Lieutenant le Grange Le we get a coffin, (*Calls.*) soldier, (*To body.*) dat's de least we can do for de old crook,

Lieutenant Chan The man was a real, heavyweight man, years to come people will say,

Mikey *enters.*

Mikey Sir, what are your orders,

Lieutenant Chan Soldier, go an find a coffin, it look as though yer was right, Major Ferret murder President Jones, we taking his body to keep in private until we can arrange a proper state funeral,

Mikey Yes, sir,

Lieutenant Chan An soldier, all that is a military secret, yer hear,

Mikey Yes, sir, a tink we out a coffins, sir,

Lieutenant Chan Go an look for one, an put in a request fer more,

Mikey Yes, sir, is that all sir, (*Salutes, goes out.*)

Lieutenant Chan Yer notice he salute,

Lieutenant le Grange Man, alright, let's go,

Lieutenant Chan Hang on yer forget something,

Lieutenant le Grange What,

Lieutenant Chan Ferret's Sergeant, Black Lightning, how we know he wasn't behind de anonymous phone call telling we de President was escaping, an not waiting out dere to waste we,

Lieutenant le Grange That's smart, you see how ycr could think when yer have to, alright a tell yer what, we better stay here, an,

Lieutenant Chan Here,

Lieutenant le Grange Yes, we keep watch, equal turns, den wen it's daylight, we drive outa here in de APC with de front an rear mounted HMG's an make we moves, what yer say,

Lieutenant Chan Here,

Lieutenant le Grange That's right, here,

Lieutenant Chan Alright, but no jokes, eh,

Lieutenant le Grange I is a big man, man, I don' make jokes,

Lieutenant Chan Where yer going,

Lieutenant le Grange To find some blankets, man,

Lieutenant Chan I'll come with yer,

Lieutenant le Grange Why, man, have a rest,

Lieutenant Chan We could continue talking,

Lieutenant le Grange What happen, yer fraid a dead body or yer don't trust me,

Lieutenant Chan No man,

Lieutenant le Grange Yer think I might go an pull some forward stroke on you, eh, like phone up Larry Roberts, an say who was responsible for de students stoning de Embassy an de North Koreans pay five thousand won, for the unshredded papers, no, man, I don't do dem kinda tings,

Lieutenant Chan How you know how much dey pay,

Lieutenant le Grange I ask for them for seven, relax man, I need you as much as you need me, a think after we stabilise the situation, you better go an lie down on a beach for a while, I could run things, (*Goes.*)

Lieutenant Chan Alright, go, go an get yer blankets, (*Turns out light, takes out pistol, cocks it, crouches, aims at doorway.*)

Lieutenant le Grange (*returns with blankets over head*) Scooby doo, where are you,

Lieutenant Chan *shoots. Dogs bark off.*

Lieutenant le Grange Oh God, oh God, Chan is me, le Grange,

More shots, dogs bark.

Alright yer Chinese mother ass, yer want ter take over, yer want power, a go give yer, power,

More shots, barks, a beat, a howl.

I also know yer was moving cocaine for dem Colombians, through dat half Spanish diplomatic courier, yer was supposed to be screwing,

More shots.

Lieutenant Chan Yes, an what about, you, you set up a weed factory an dat half Indian dog yer buy all de jewellery for, give it ter she Barbados beach bum ter buy my coke,

More shots, barks, a beat, **Mikey** *comes to door, unlocks.*

Mikey Psst, psst, sir, sir, yer alright sir,

Lieutenant Chan Yes, put on the light, soldier,

Mikey (*does*) What, yes, sir, wat happen, sir,

Lieutenant Chan It look like there's been another accident, soldier,

Mikey Yes sir,

Lieutenant Chan As you know there have been several assassination attempts on Lieutenant le Grange an myself, by dem right-wing Portuguese half creoles,

Mikey No sir,

Lieutenant Chan Well, I'm glad to hear that, because it's for officers' eyes only, but anyhow we was expecting another one, an when Lieutenant le Grange enter with the grey an white striped blanket over his head I thought it was one a dem, an shoot him by mistake,

Mikey Yes, sir,

Lieutenant Chan An soldier all that is military secret, too,

Mikey Yes, sir, what to do with de body sir,

Lieutenant Chan Drag it over in the corner an put a blanket over it,

Mikey Yes, sir, (*Does.*)

Lieutenant Chan I going to get my men, we coming back to take de President body to de cathedral, watch me, we go show the world if is one ting Trinis know how to do is throw funeral, cover me,

Mikey Yes, sir,

Places blanket on **Lieutenant Chan***'s shoulders,* **Lieutenant Chan** *shrugs it off.*

Lieutenant Chan Me back man, me back, you sure you is a Trinidadian,

They go.

Scene Six

A blood-splattered wall. Sounds of firing squad marching on. Enter **Lieutenant Chan** *followed by* **Black Lightning** *reading book.*

Lieutenant Chan (*goes to wall, lines up with squad, off*) Yes, here,

Black Lightning *goes to spot.*

Lieutenant Chan (*takes out warrant, reads*) Fitzroy Emmanuel Allyne, Sergeant, serial number three four seven, PE instructor, regiment of the Republic of Trinidad an Tobago, also known as Black Lightning, by order of the President an Commander in Chief of the armed forces, you have been tried according to section 47, paragraph nine, of the constitution of the said Republic, and found guilty of the crime of murder an treason, you are hereby sentenced to die by firing squad, in accordance with section nine, paragraph seven, of the agreement between the armed forces and the non-commissioned officers industrial association, on this day Thursday, eighteenth July, in the year of our Lord, nineteen hundred and ninety one, an may God have mercy on your soul. Signed General Robert Chan, President of the Republic of Trinidad an Tobago, (*Offers blindfold.*) yer want dese,

Black Lightning No, tank you sir,

Lieutenant Chan Squad (*Steps back, raises hand.*)

Black Lightning Sir,

Lieutenant Chan (*drops arm*) What,

Black Lightning Yer forget something, sir,

Lieutenant Chan What's that,

Black Lightning Yer ferget ter ask me if a had a last wish,

Lieutenant Chan What,

Black Lightning A said yer forget,

Lieutenant Chan Yes, yes, a know what yer say, but that does only happen in Hollywood man, when the hero, this is Trinidad man, so leggo dat, squad, ready, (*Raises arm.*)

Black Lightning Dat's not true sir,

Lieutenant Chan (*lowers arm*) What,

Black Lightning It's in here sir,

Lieutenant Chan What is,

Black Lightning De last request, sir, here, (*Shows book.*) section seven, paragraph nine, of the agreement between the armed forces of the Republic of Trinidad an Tobago an the non-commissioned officers association, no non-commissioned officer shall be executed by firing squad, unless offered the request of a last wish, sub-section 12, paragraph 84, blindfolds, red paper hearts pinned on the chest, a king sized low tar Broadway cigarette notwithstanding, such a request not to be unreasonably withheld but binding on the mutual agreement of both parties concerned,

Lieutenant Chan (*grabs book*) Le me see dat, dis is a joke, who negotiate this,

Black Lightning You sir, an Sergeant Lucas, Francis an Boysie, if yer ask dem a sure de squad, would agree,

Lieutenant Chan Alright, what is yer last request,

Black Lightning A king sized low tar Broadway, sir,

Lieutenant Chan Alright, any a all yer have a cigarette, give him one, alright den one a all yer go an find one, (*To* **Sergeant**.) alright relax, yer see how much trouble yer causing, if even dey was going to feel sorry fer yer an miss, now yer gone,

Black Lightning It's the rules sir,

Lieutenant le Grange *runs on with piece of cigarette*,

Lieutenant Chan What is this,

Soldier It was Sergeant Lucas's last one, sir, but when he hear it was for Black Lightning he break the neck,

Lieutenant Chan Go an find a whole one, a sure it have a sub-section to a sub-section that it have to be a whole one, right,

Black Lightning *shrugs.* **Soldier** *runs off.*

Lieutenant Chan So tell me ner, all them stories I hear bout you is true,

Black Lightning Well, sir, it depends on which stories yer mean, some is an some isn't,

Lieutenant Chan How yer mean,

Black Lightning Well sir, if you trace a man's action back to its original source, you will most likely discover he was a mere tool in the hands, of sociological, economic, genetic an more powerful forces,

Lieutenant Chan Like what,

Black Lightning But sir,

Lieutenant Chan Go on, I'm interested,

Black Lightning Well yer see, sir, it's like dis, sir, take me for instance, ever since I was a small boy, I wanted to be a soldier, now where I get dat from, I was too small to go to cinema, an I en read no comics, so where I learn dat from, is de genes, someting in de genes I was carrying was telling me dem tings, ter pick up a piece of stick an say bang, bang, bang, yer see wat a mean, genetic, right,

Lieutenant Chan Right,

Black Lightning But yer see wat happen when yer start ter play someting, yer get to like it, take Kelvin Wong Chong, his father had de only Chinese shop for miles, he was king, he used to hand out casa balls an lollipop like dey was Spanish treasure, an is only because both a we had mumps I get to play with him, yer see de economic side coming up,

Lieutenant Chan Right,

Black Lightning Hang on the socio, coming too, when we was playing stick-em-up behind he father flour bags, I creep on him an capture him, an lock him in de dark bathroom, an de more he beg is de more I tell him, how much scorpion an rattle snake was in dere, yer see his economic power was forcing me to act in an anti-social manner, the socio, a was telling yer bout,

Lieutenant Chan Yes, yes, but what about,

Black Lightning The more powerful forces,

Lieutenant Chan Yes, tell me bout them, I,

Soldier *runs on holding cigarette,* **Lieutenant Chan** *ignores him.*

Black Lightning Well, them is serious tings yer talking bout,

Soldier Sir,

Lieutenant Chan What is it, soldier,

Soldier Sir, a find a cigarette, sir,

Lieutenant Chan Well, yer can't see we talking, look him dey, give it to him,

Soldier Yes, sir, (*Does.*)

Black Lightning A need a light,

Lieutenant Chan Don't tell me yer didn't bring a light, an you interrupt us fer dat, how you tink he go light it, your face an my ass,

Soldier You didn't say notting bout no light sir,

Lieutenant le Grange Well a telling you now, go an find a light den,

Soldier *walks off. Stewps*.

Lieutenant Chan A sorry bout dat, we not getting quality recruits like you, dese days,

Black Lightning Some a dem not too bad, dey just need,

Lieutenant Chan Forget bout dem, go on with the forces, I hear dey have men, who could kill yer for three days an bring you back alive as dey slave, as walking zombies,

Black Lightning Oh, dem, right, right, dem tings as well, yes, well yer see dem is harder to define, you en go find dem in no book, dey more unscientific, underground, more,

Lieutenant Chan Powerful,

Black Lightning Right, you can't play with dem tings, it might begin simple an ordinary, but den it turn out, boof, yer know wat a mean,

Lieutenant Chan Yes, yes, like,

Black Lightning Yer sure yer don't have a light on yer,

Lieutenant Chan No, no, a sure,

Black Lightning Is alright, a could wait, take when I an Assistant Commissioner Blake went on a customs raid on Chin Loy shop, he tought he had life all cut an dried, he tought he could just walk in Chin Loy shop an check he receipts an he goods, alright we catch him with forty bags

of pure opium, but dat wasn't it, Chin Loy tell he wife ter
cook some chow mein, an de next ting I know is a bottle a
Johnny Walker white label hit de table, we clean dat off, den
a bottle of Dubonnet arrive, we kill dat, after we destroy de
chow mein, an two more bottles of someting, we driving back
to town, on de coconut road, Assistant Commissioner Blake
suddenly decide he want to swim in Manzanilla waters, so
I say no, sir, le we wait until we reach, Nariva, I know de
waters was safer dere, but he say no, stop de car, he want to
swim now, de man, run out de car, before he hit de water he
was naked, de first breaker hit him, right side, de second hit
him starboard, he was reeling, so I undress an dash in to save
him, an manage to grab he hair, but it was a wig, all de time
de man was wearing a wig I never know dat, den a breaker
hit me, port an starboard too, an I too was reeling, I know I
was in trouble, an I is a strong swimmer,

Lieutenant Chan Yes, yes,

Black Lightning Is den I hear de first voice, it was a woman's,
just like me mother,

Lieutenant Chan What she say,

Black Lightning Let go,

Lieutenant Chan Da is all, let go,

Black Lightning No, wait ner,

Lieutenant Chan Right, right, sorry,

Black Lightning Where's de fire,

Lieutenant Chan A send for it,

Black Lightning Is a joke, a mean what's yer hurry,

Lieutenant Chan Oh, right, right, sorry,

Black Lightning Den de second voice come on, dat was a
woman's too,

Lieutenant Chan Not yer mother's,

Black Lightning No, me Auntie Thelma's, an she I had to listen to,

Lieutenant Chan What she say,

Black Lightning She say, boy listen to yer mother ner, listen to yer mother,

Lieutenant Chan So what yer do,

Black Lightning Dis time I in de middle of de sea, de undertow carrying me out, further an further, Assistant Commissioner Blake gone, den me mother voice come back on de line,

Lieutenant Chan Wat she say,

Black Lightning She say, boy why yer head so hard like a coconut, let go, float like a empty coconut bobbing on the waves, an I felt every fibre of dat coconut was de fibres of my body, I could taste de jelly dat was in dat coconut, the milk, an de knowledge dat my kernel could be grated an made into sugar cakes that schoolboys would snatch an wrestle over, my husk could be beaten in a four four Yoruba rhythm by a master mattress maker, for lovers to snuggle in,

Lieutenant Chan Yes, yes, then what,

Black Lightning Then a coast guard patrol boat fish me out, still holding Assistant Commissioner Blake's wig in me hands,

Lieutenant Chan I see, I see, so wat you trying to tell me is you, innocent, you wasn't going to waste me,

Black Lightning Sir, yer miss de whole point of de story, sir,

Lieutenant Chan Alright, a sorry, hit me, wat's de point of de story?

Black Lightning Is you ask me to tell yer, yer know,

Lieutenant Chan Alright, a said a was sorry, tell me,

Black Lightning Dat soldier taking he time, I dying for a smoke,

Lieutenant Chan Yes, yes, go on ner,

Black Lightning A tink a go wait till he come, de nicotine does give me a lift, an yer go get a better story,

Lieutenant Chan Yes,

Black Lightning Yer see de best bit is, the answer to man's search for total an complete control of the forces of nature, is,

Lieutenant Chan Hold on, wait a minute, (*Calls.*) what's keeping that light, de light dat dog face went for, no, not a bulb, a light, light as in fire, yer know wat dat means, fire, fire,

Shots. **Black Lightning** *falls.*

Lieutenant Chan No, no, fire as in light, (*Runs to body.*) the answer, what's the answer, (*Puts ear to* **Black Lightning**'s *mouth.*) that's the answer, fire, fire, (*a bucket of water is thrown at him.*)

Scene Seven

The cell.

President *is asleep, laughing.* **Mikey** *enters. Goes to* **President**.

Mikey Sir, sir, wake up sir, the Americans, the news from the Embassy is not good, dey,

President Yes, yes, what, what they say,

Mikey De Americans, playing some kinda game yer know, sir,

President Why, what they say,

Mikey Well, she went through Checkpoint Atilla an went straight for the library as a told her, an started dusting the

Hispanic section, an looking round for who could be Mister Larry Roberts an there was only one feller there, so she went straight up an told him,

President What,

Mikey She have a message from the President of her country, for him,

President Good for her,

Mikey Then she tell him, that you was alive an in here, an the regime crumbling an that under no circumstances they must grant diplomatic recognition,

President Good, good, yes, she did well, then what,

Mikey Then he asked her, how does he know she's who she say she is, an not working for some, Chekhov an Lorca,

President The Havana controller, for the Southern Region, an his KGB boss, good poker players, but they like the ladies too much,

Mikey An knowing that if Uncle Sam withhold diplomatic recognition the entire economic infrastructure of the island, will collapse, which will give them the perfect excuse to kick Uncle Sam out, which means they will, she told him, look, Mister, she don't know bout them tings, she only get to fifth standard in school, she miss free-hand writing an since the coup I get prison duty, an I give she the message, to give to him,

President What he say,

Mikey He said, all he years in de region, he never heard a story like that, an it's too Goddamned simple to be a trick,

President Then what,

Mikey Then he told her he was getting back to Puerto Rico, to recommend a hold on withholding recognition, but, that's what a been trying to tell yer, sir, he say, they say, they want proof, proof that yer still alive, an they want yer at the Embassy back gate by sunset, tonight, if not they going ahead, sir,

President An how I getting outa here,

Mikey I don't know, sir,

President An how we getting past A an C companies,

Mikey I don't,

President An how we know we can trust the Americans,

Mikey Sir, I,

President So, de Americans backing Ferret, so wat do we do,

Mikey We have to get you out a here, sir, Lieutenant Chan coming back for you an we just pick up on de grapevine frequency Major Ferret, on de way here with a armoured column, everything breaking down outside dey, the soldiers gone freaky, some a dem painting up they face an saying, call me Geronimo, an snake eye, even the North Korean instructors gone back, some officers stop talking to other officers, just cussing they mother an browbeating them interlectually, in front of the men, an ordering up, all the M16 ammo, an saltfish field rations, people barricading off parts of the city, an charging taxes, declaring them independent republics, calling dem Lumumbaville an Dodge City, soon they go, order soldiers to fire on soldiers an I don't want to be around when that happen, sir,

President Alright,

Mikey De Sergeant an de fellers, agree to support us, an a think a know a way to get you outa here, but if a tell yer, yer go only give me some long technical argument, just get ready to move, (*Goes out, enters pushing straw laundry basket.*) come sir, get in, (*Uncovering.*)

President What's that for,

Mikey Is Lieutenant Chan give me de idea, sir, soon as he say coffin, a say da is it, dey was saving dis fer you, da is how we getting you outa here, a back de Landrover into de doorway, load you up, an we,

President What happen, you couldn't find a trunk or something,

Mikey Yer see what a tell yer,

President Alright wait, I have a better idea, why don't we put le Grange in here, I put on his uniform an we cruise outa here, by the time dey find out, we,

Mikey Not bad, but a still tink

President Trust me, I didn't become President by guess, you know,

Undressing body.

Mikey (*into walkie talkie/corridor*) Alright, baker one to baker two, over, Sarge, Michael here, all yer secure Gordon Street gate yet, over,

Sarge Michael who,

Mikey Jones, Sarge, me, President guard, a just talk to you, man, over, all yer ready, we,

Sarge Or, is you, right, right, a wasn't sure, no, not yet,

Mikey What's de problem, over,

Sarge Well, it's like dis, yer see, some a de fellers, having doubts an second thoughts about de feasibility of de operation, over,

Mikey Like what, over,

Sarge Like what in it for dem, over, after all, a mean ter say, we putting we life on de line on behalf of dis enterprise, an we could get serious damage for dis business, supposing, just supposing all yer succeed, wat in it fer we, except couple gold medal, gold ribbon an gold,

Mikey Sarge, man, dis is life an death we talking bout, here man, we country,

Sarge Yer still dere, over,

President Sergeant, this is President Jones, I, personally,

Sarge Yer still dere, over,

Mikey (to **President**) Sir, let me, alright. (*To* **Sarge**.) What all yer want, over,

Sarge A go have to call you back on that, over out,

Mikey Sarge, we don't,

President The little crooks,

Mikey They is only soldiers, sir, you leave Sarge to me, I,

President I didn't know your name was Jones,

Mikey Yes, sir, a didn't tell you, my mother say it was my real name, me father was just, me stepfather, an, (*Dressing.*)

President Small world,

Mikey Yes,

President What you think,

Mikey With your reputation, it's possible,

President Anything is possible, how a look,

Mikey Like a General, sir,

President Well, let's behave like one, talk to them, always keep talking,

Mikey Sarge, this is Michael, over, what going on, all yer ready to resume negotiations, over,

Sarge Who's dat,

Mikey Michael, a just talk to you, man, yer naming yer price,

Sarge Or you, right, right, yes, just checking, well, the position is dis, we in deadlock, de fellers from Arawak platoon, want honourable discharge from the regiment, tirty acres a land on de Gran Couva hills, some Massey-Ferguson tractor, an nobody trouble them, at all, an de fellers from Carib platoon want de same honourable discharge from the regiment but on three star General, pension, Mirama Nightclub on Marine Square, an de one in San Fernando, an nobody trouble them at all, but we car come to a democratic decision, over,

Mikey Alright, alright, granted, all yer have it, whatever all yer want, all yer, (*Shots.*) what's de shooting, over,

Sarge We try to convince the boys from Arawak platoon, but two a dem make a break through de gate, so yer agree terms,

Mikey Yes, yes, alright, hold yer fire, but we have a slight change of plan, me, Lieutenant le Grange, an de President driving out to find,

Sarge Hole on a minute, you tink you catching me wit dat,

Mikey What yer mean,

Sarge You an le Grange drive outa here, de President stays,

Mikey What yer mean, as hostage,

Sarge Security, you tink I born yesterday,

Mikey Yer is a hard man, Sarge, look after him, yer know,

Sarge Like a baby, alright, all yer come out fast, an no freaky business,

President Where you learn to do that,

Mikey Do what sir, now Mister President, what are your orders,

President We are going to the cathedral an present myself to the people, they will protect me, when they hear I dead an lying in state, the whole island go flock there, when they see a alive, well, the coup over, they wouldn't dare touch me, (*Going.*) come, let's go and clean up the country, was your mother, a brown skin girl, with a house on Charlotte Street, (*Off.*)

Sarge Sir, yer dere sir, tell Michael an Lieutenant le Grange
not to come out, an yer better take cover, Major Ferret an
he men arriving an taking up defensive positions behind
de petrol tanks, de ones dat was leaking last night, an
Corporal Jadoo was suppose to fix, but he couldn't because
he boyfriend turn up an, wait, now Lieutenant Chan an he
men arrive, an offloading with grenade launchers, an taking
up offensive positions, Lieutenant Chan come out with a white
flag, Major Ferret come out, dey stop, dey talking, dey talking,
dey laughing, dey laughing, Major Ferret take out a big cigar
an offer it to Chan, dey lighting up, no, no, no, all yer go back,
go back,

Sound of explosions.

Scene Eight

As Scene One

*There are two workmen in overalls holding brooms like rifles at
the coffin.*

Workman 1 A hear some reactionary elements, aided an
abetted by South African mercenaries tried to rescue him
from de people's custody an a Uzi machine pistol fall out
of a sleeping sentry hand an start firing by itself an one of
de bullets hit a nail on a beam over he head an on de nail
was a old iron anchor an dat fall on he head, an wen dey
searched de body, dey found, twelve centigrammes of cocaine,
in plastic packets that was addressed, to the Lady Pembroke
Handicapped Children's Home, four dozen porno videos that
was even banned in Amsterdam, seven uncut diamonds, a piece
of string, an a shrunken head in the right hand breast, pocket
of his Saville Row suit,

Workman 2 You believe dat,

Workman 1 No, dey lie, what a big man like he doing with
a piece of string in he pocket,

They move on.

Workman 2 Yer going back to work,

Workman 1 No, man, yer know how much mess, dem people does make at funerals, all dem sweet drink bottles an roti paper, let de army clean up, le we call a emergency meeting of de 5th Battalion of the People's Sanitation Squadron an go to de rum shop an watch de finals of de Hungarian women volleyball finals, boy, they shorts, short,

Off, behind them, two nuns.

Nun 1 (*they both make sign of cross*) Well girl, the Lord give an He take it away, what a waste,

Nun 2 Such a good man,

Nun 1 Such a fine man, what a waste, a good six-inch man, like dat,

Nun 2 Only six, an how come dey say he had children all over de place,

Nun 1 Not six long, six around, girl, if a tell yer how long they say, (*Whispers.*)

Nun 2 Santa Maria, how you know, you measure it,

Nun 1 An it had a bend in de middle, de weight yer know, an a full grown coral snake tattooed round it, in colour,

Nun 2 No, not a full grown one, what woman could take that, I en taking dat, I would say thank you, Mister, a like yer Mercedes with de soft top, a like yer disco pose, but I en taking dat, not me, keep it for one a dem American tourist carnival time, eh,

Nun 1 Is de same wit me, girl, I would say, sorry, Mister, keep yer weekends at yer beach house, keep yer gold bracelet an yer diamond earrings, but me doctor say, me heart can't take de strain,

Nun 2 Dey say, a bullet miss it by inches, so dey take dat as a sign an cut it off an pickling it in a jar, with vinegar,

Nun 1 Where dey keeping it,

Nun 2 De Natural History Museum fighting with de Agricultural Department over it, but a tink dey might send it to UNESCO for safe keeping,

Nun 1 Why not, is part of we history,

Nuns *move on. Sirens. Curtain.*